Blues, Jazz, Rock & Rags
Book 2

T0081929

12
ORIGINAL PIANO SOLOS
by Jennifer and Mike Watts

ISBN 978-1-61780-663-6

HAL•LEONARD®
CORPORATION
7777 W. BLUEMOUND RD. P.O. BOX 13819 MILWAUKEE, WI 53213

In Australia Contact:
Hal Leonard Australia Pty. Ltd.
4 Lentara Court
Cheltenham, Victoria, 3192 Australia
Email: ausadmin@halleonard.com.au

Visit Hal Leonard Online at
www.halleonard.com

Contents

Charley B's Disco

By Jennifer and Mike Watts

Driving (♩ = 116)

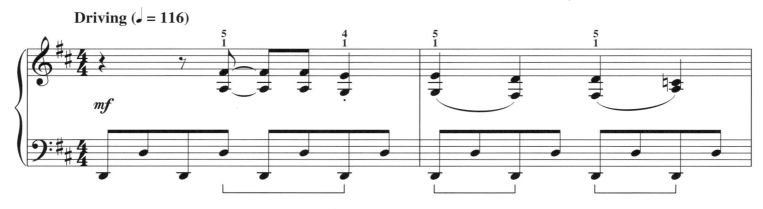

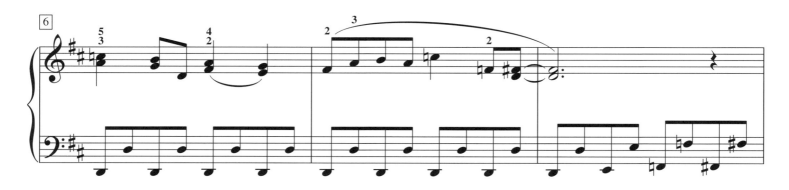

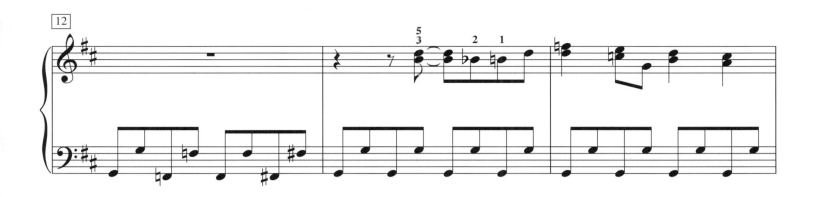

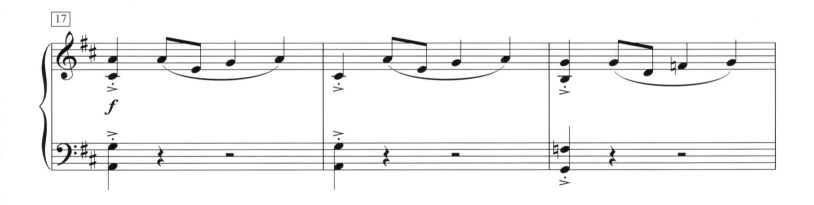

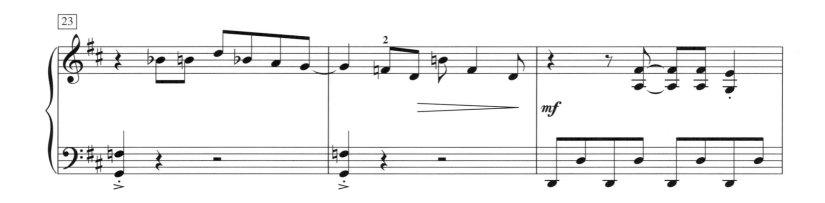

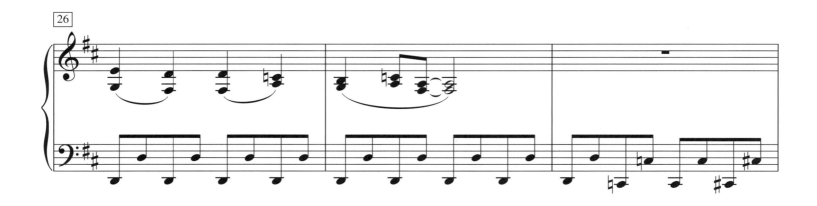

Chasin' Monsters

By Jennifer and Mike Watts

Freakishly funny! (♩ = 132)

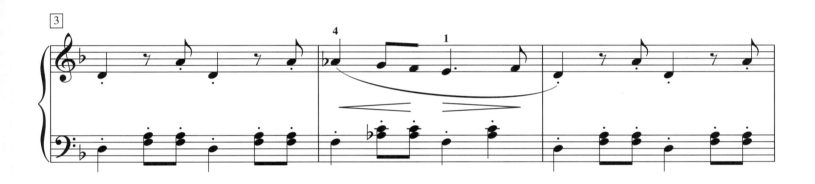

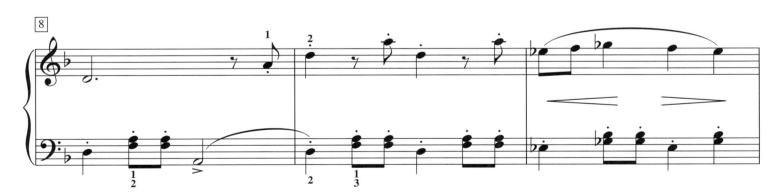

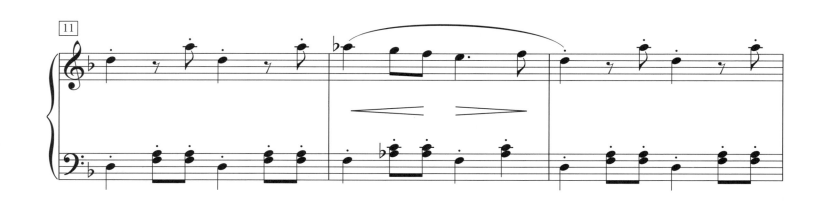

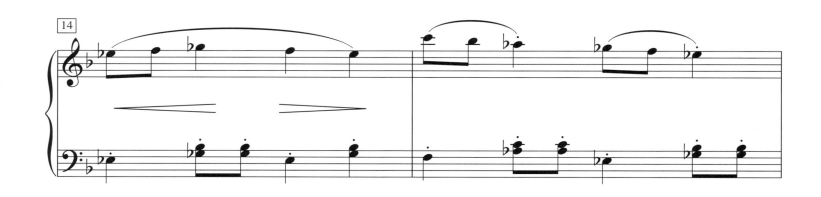

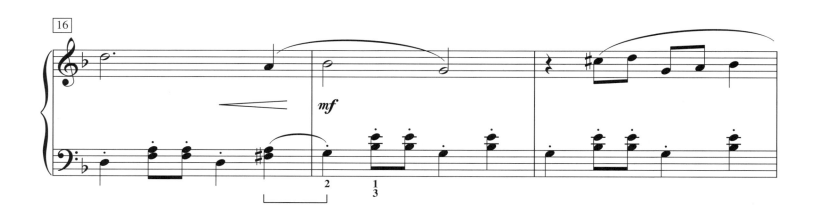

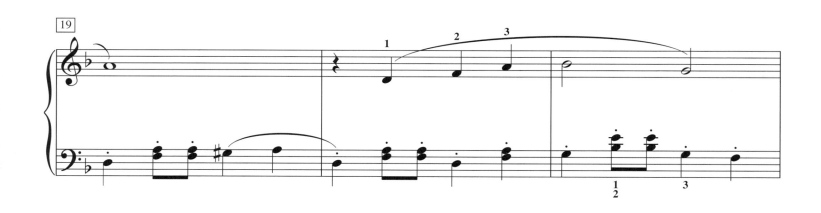

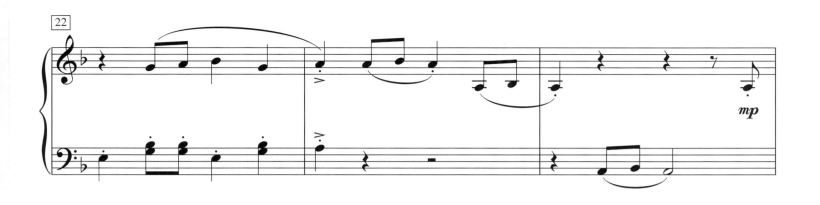

The Doctor Is In

By Jennifer and Mike Watts

Cajun fun! (♩ = 126)

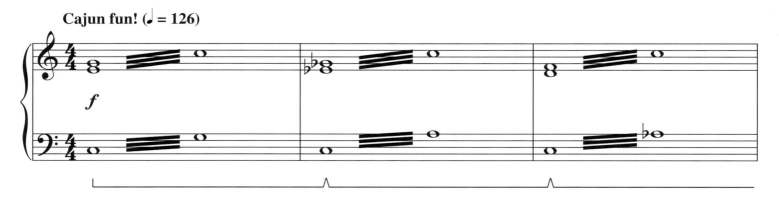

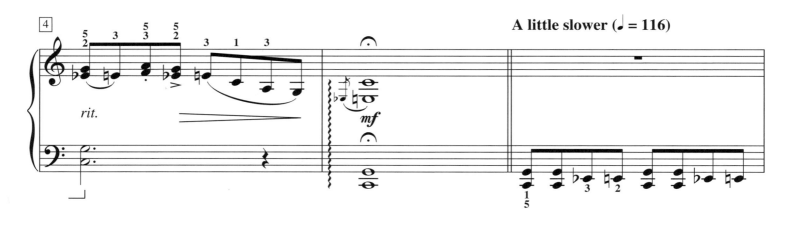

A little slower (♩ = 116)

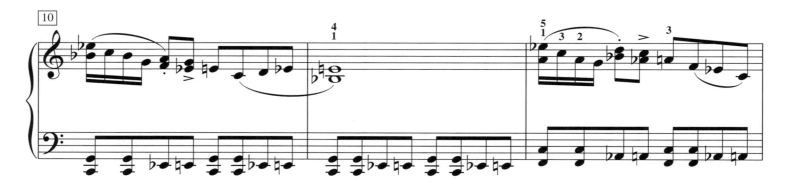

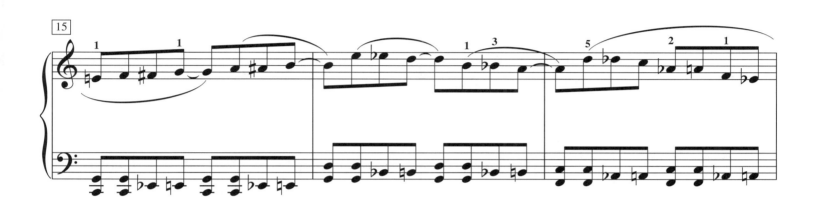

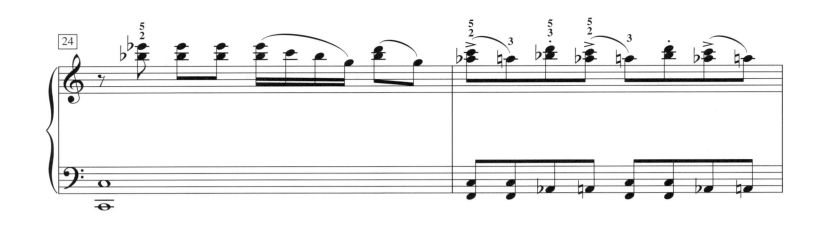

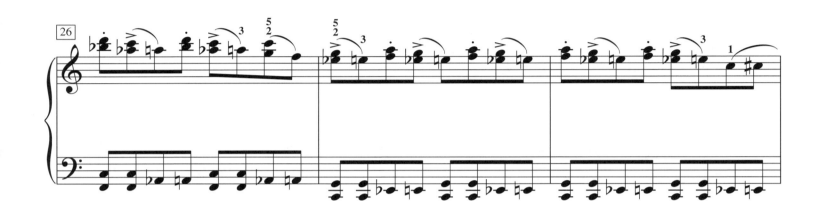

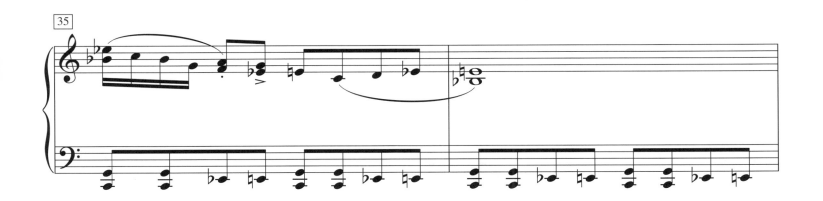

Fancy Blues

By Jennifer and Mike Watts

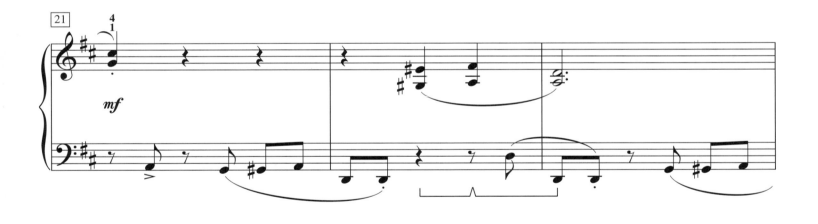

15

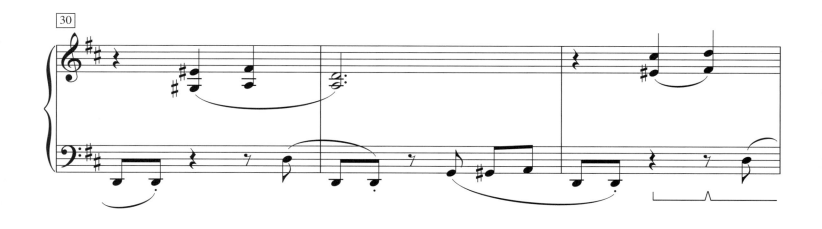

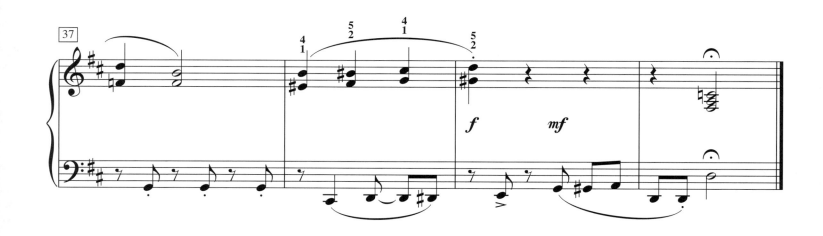

Klumzy Kangaroo

By Jennifer and Mike Watts

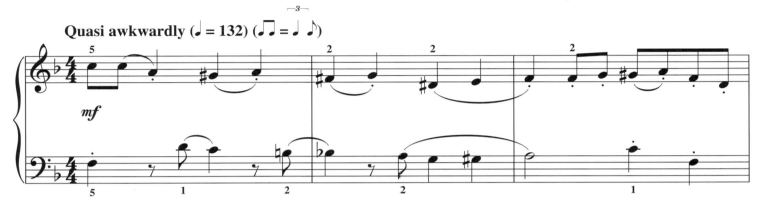

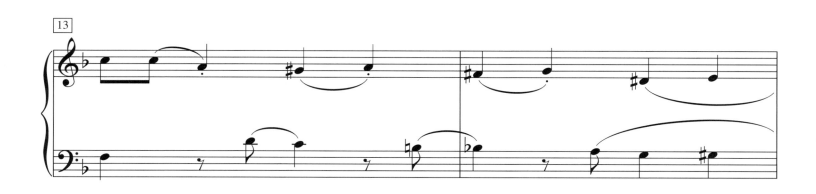

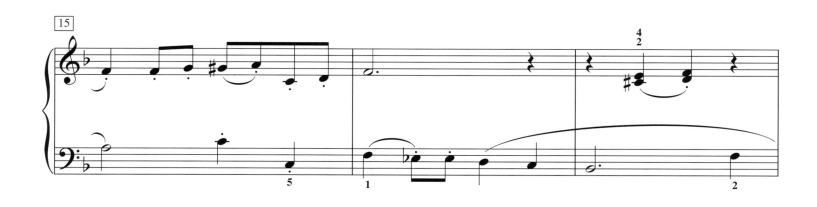

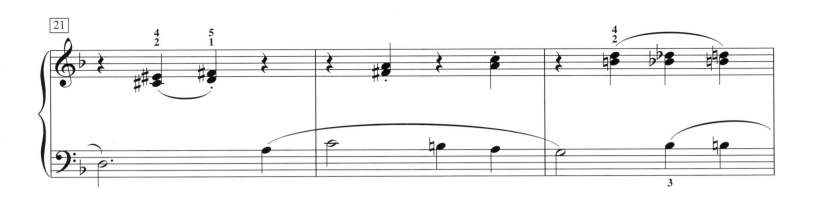

Jammin' Away

By Jennifer and Mike Watts

Nobody Doesn't Like Jerry Lee

By Jennifer and Mike Watts

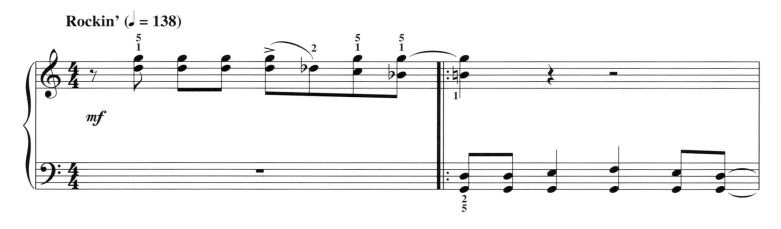

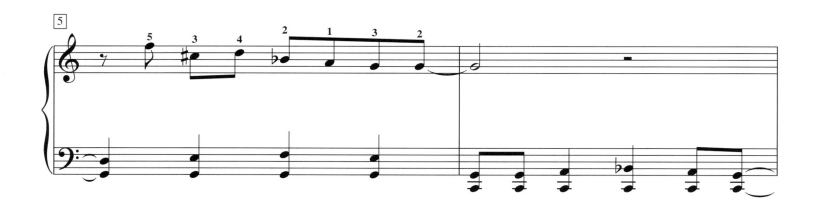

Pretty Slick

By Jennifer and Mike Watts

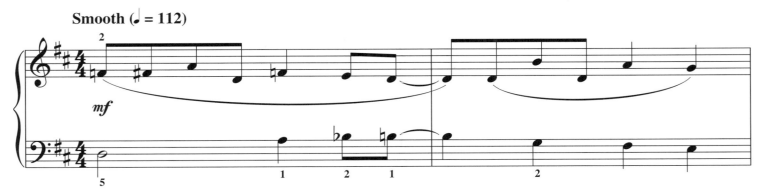

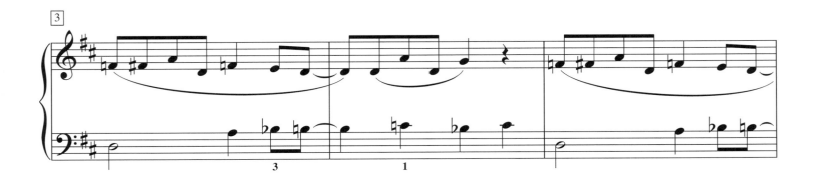

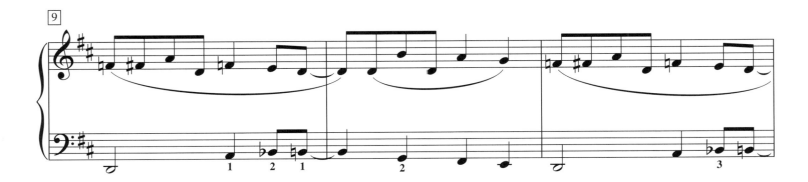

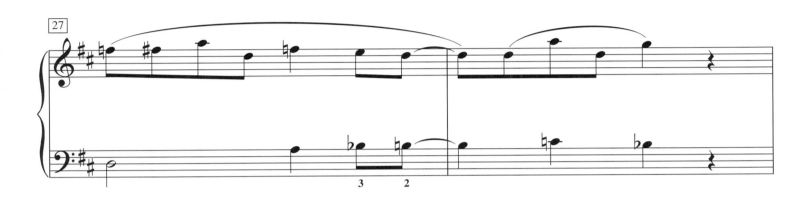

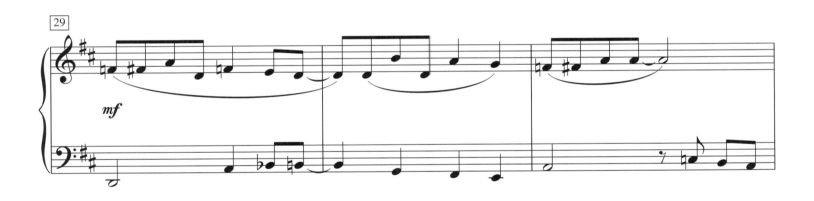

Remember When

By Jennifer and Mike Watts

Dolce (♩ = 80)

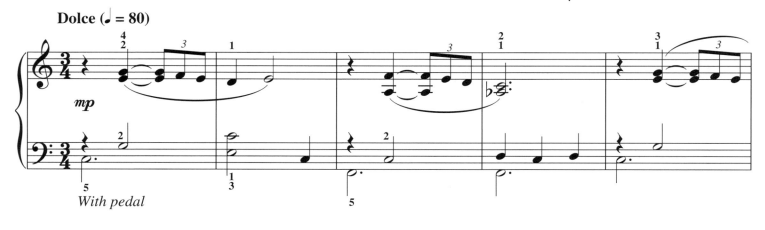

mp

With pedal

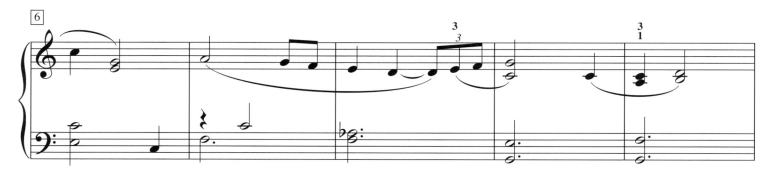

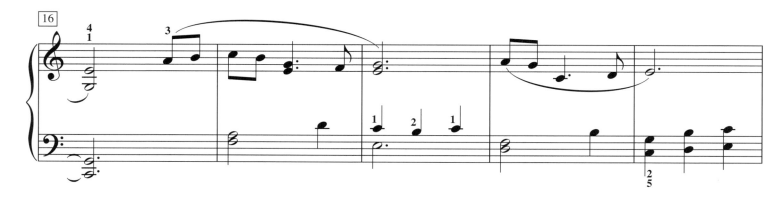

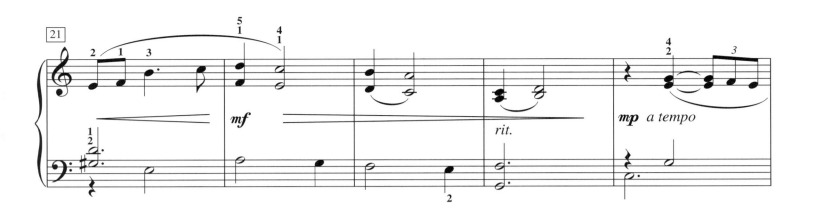

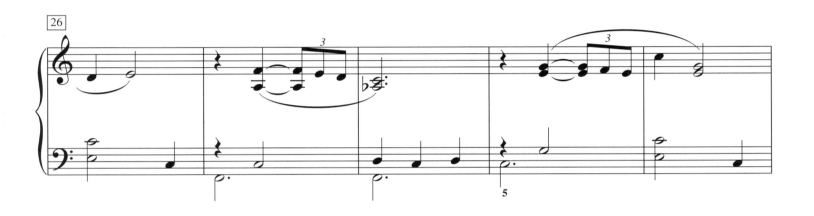

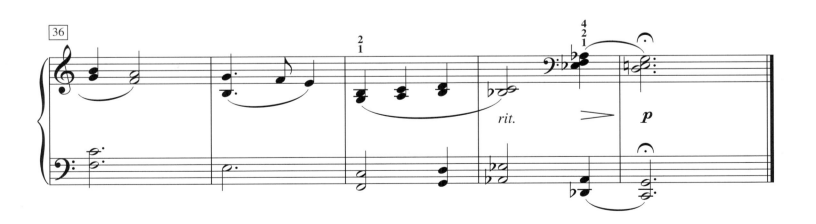

Surf's Up!

Secondo

By Jennifer and Mike Watts

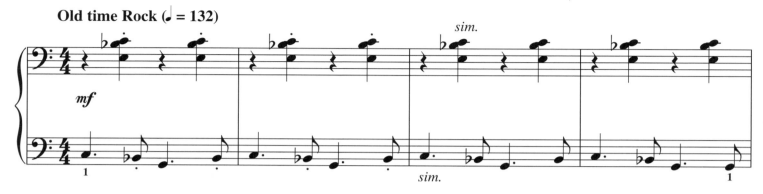

Surf's Up!

Primo

By Jennifer and Mike Watts

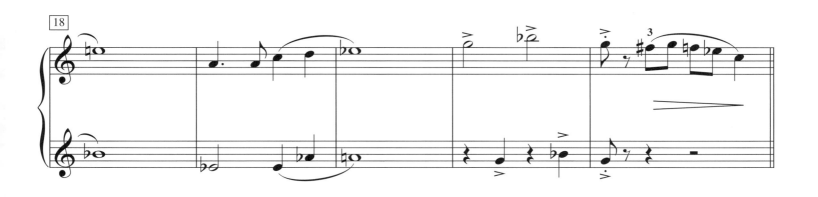

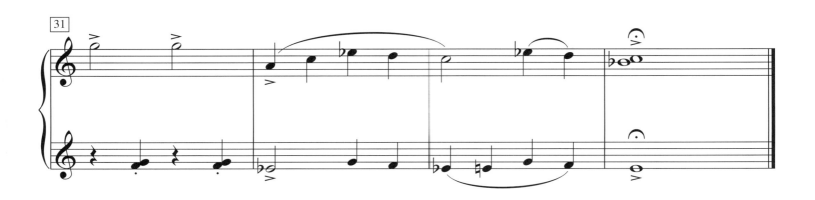

Swingin' Rag

By Jennifer and Mike Watts

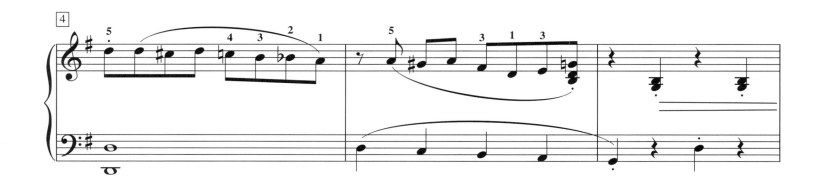

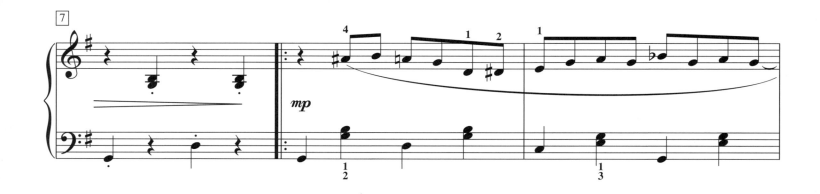

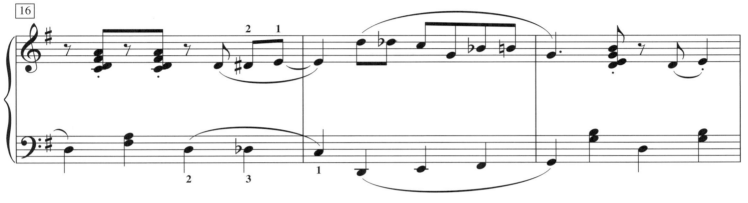

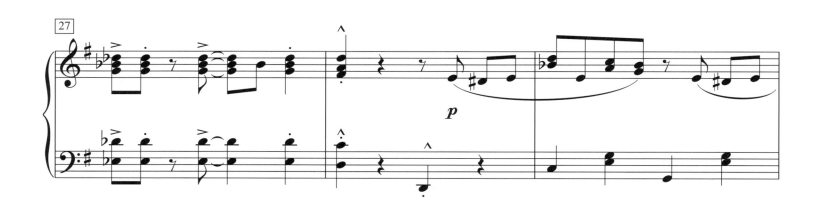

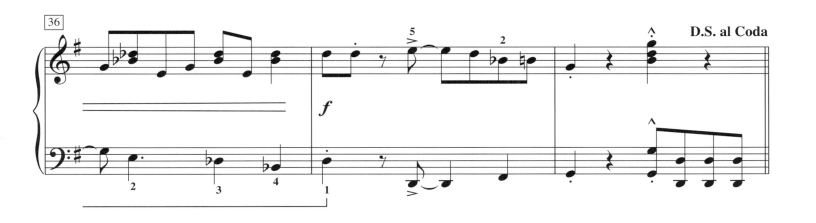

D.S. al Coda

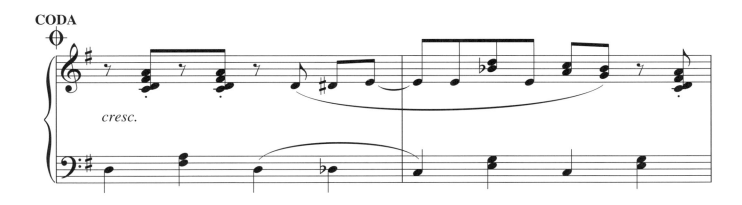

CODA

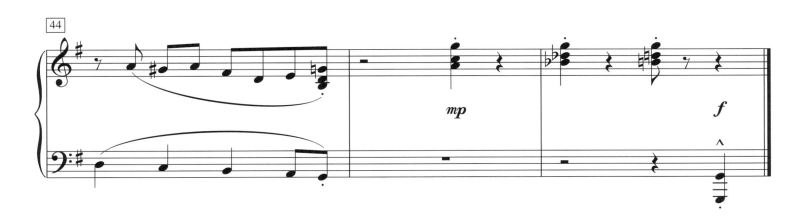

Where'd They Go

By Jennifer and Mike Watts

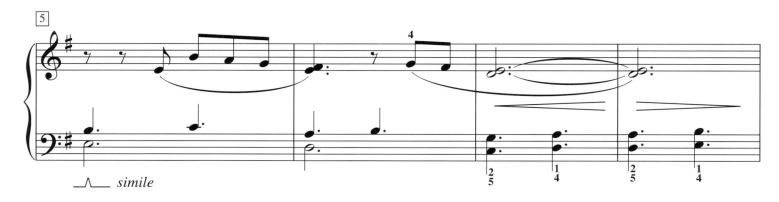

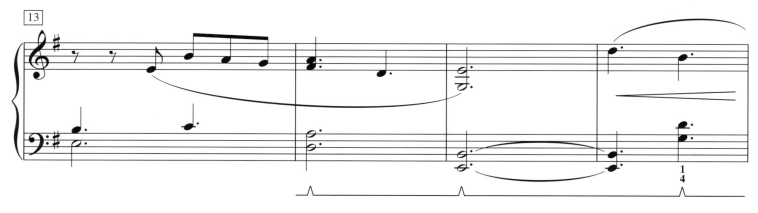

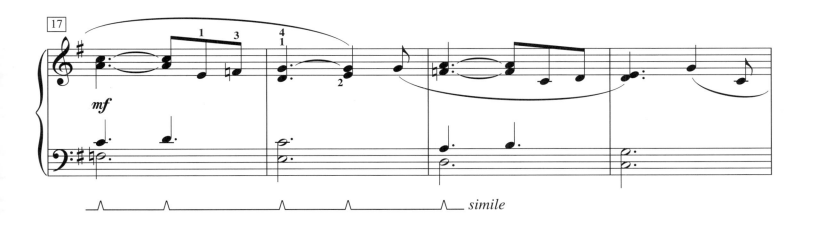

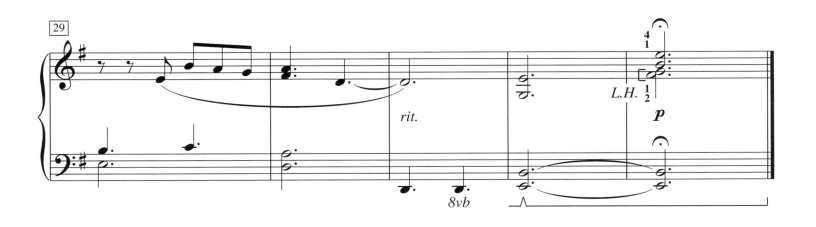

POPULAR SONGS

HAL LEONARD STUDENT PIANO LIBRARY

The **Hal Leonard Student Piano Library** has great songs, and you will find all your favorites here: Disney classics, Broadway and movie favorites, and today's top hits. These graded collections are skillfully and imaginatively arranged for students and pianists at every level, from elementary solos with teacher accompaniments to sophisticated piano solos for the advancing pianist.

The Beatles
arr. Eugénie Rocherolle

Intermediate piano solos. Songs: *Can't Buy Me Love • Get Back • Here Comes the Sun • Martha My Dear • Michelle • Ob-La-Di, Ob-La-Da • Revolution • Yesterday.*

00296649 Correlates with HLSPL Level 5.........$10.99

Broadway Hits
arr. Carol Klose

Early-Intermediate/Intermediate piano solos. Songs: *Beauty and the Beast • Circle of Life • Do-Re-Mi • It's a Grand Night for Singing • The Music of the Night • Tomorrow • Where Is Love? • You'll Never Walk Alone.*

00296650 Correlates with HLSPL Levels 4/5 .....$7.99

Chart Hits
arr. Mona Rejino

8 pop favorites carefully arranged at an intermediate level. Songs: *Bad Day • Boston • Everything • February Song • Home • How to Save a Life • Put Your Records On • What Hurts the Most.*

00296710 Correlates with HLSPL Level 5 ....$7.99

Christmas Cheer
arr. Phillip Keveren

Early Intermediate level. For 1 Piano/4 Hands. Songs: *Caroling, Caroling • The Christmas Song • It Must Have Been the Mistletoe • It's Beginning to Look Like Christmas • Rudolph the Red-Nosed Reindeer • You're All I Want for Christmas.*

00296616 Correlates with HLSPL Level 4...........$6.95

Christmas Time Is Here
arr. Eugénie Rocherolle

Intermediate level. For 1 piano/4 hands. Songs: *Christmas Time Is Here • Feliz Navidad • Here Comes Santa Claus (Right Down Santa Claus Lane) • I'll Be Home for Christmas • Little Saint Nick • White Christmas.*

00296614 Correlates with HLSPL Level 5...........$7.99

Classic Joplin Rags
arr. Fred Kern

Intermediate/Late Intermediate. Six quintessential Joplin rags arranged by Fred Kern: *Bethena (Concert Waltz) • The Entertainer • Maple Leaf Rag • Pineapple Rag • Pleasant Moments (Ragtime Waltz) • Swipesy (Cake Walk).*

00296743 Correlates with HLSPL Level 5 ....$6.95

FOR MORE INFORMATION, SEE YOUR LOCAL MUSIC DEALER, OR WRITE TO:

HAL•LEONARD®
CORPORATION

7777 W. BLUEMOUND RD. P.O. BOX 13819 MILWAUKEE, WI 53213

Prices, contents and availability subject to change without notice. Prices may vary outside the U.S.

Disney characters and artwork © Disney Enterprises, Inc.

Contemporary Movie Hits
arr. by Carol Klose, Jennifer Linn and Wendy Stevens

Six blockbuster movie favorites arranged for intermediate-level piano solo: *Bella's Lullaby • Breaking Free • Dawn • Georgiana • He's a Pirate • That's How You Know.*

00296780 Correlates with HLSPL Level 5..........$8.99

Contemporary Pop Hits
arr. Wendy Stevens

Seven top hits your late elementary students will love to learn! Includes: All the Right Moves (OneRepublic) • Baby (Justin Bieber) • Breakout (Miley Cyrus) • Hey, Soul Sister (Train) • Love Story (Taylor Swift) • Lovebug (Jonas Brothers) • When I Look at You (Miley Cyrus).

00296836 Correlates with HLSPL Level 3........$8.99

Current Hits
arr. Mona Rejino

Seven of today's hottest hits by artists such as Coldplay, Daughtry and Leona Lewis arranged as intermediate solos. Includes: *Apologize • Bleeding Love • Bubbly • Love Song • No One • Viva La Vida • What About Now.*

00296768 Correlates with HLSPL Level 5..........$8.99

Disney Favorites
arr. Phillip Keveren

Late-Elementary/Early-Intermediate piano solos. Songs: *Beauty and the Beast • Circle of Life • A Dream Is a Wish Your Heart Makes • I'm Late; Little April Shower • A Whole New World (Aladdin's Theme) • You Can Fly! • You'll Be in My Heart.*

00296647 Correlates with HLSPL Levels 3/4 .....$9.99

Disney Film Favorites
arr. Mona Rejino

Students of all ages will delight in Mona Rejino's intermediate arrangements of eight beloved Disney classics: *Cruella De Vil • Friend like Me • Go the Distance • God Help the Outcasts • Scales and Arpeggios • True Love's Kiss • When She Loved Me • You Are the Music in Me.*

00296809 Correlates with HLSPL Level 5....... $10.99

Getting to Know You – Rodgers & Hammerstein Favorites

Illustrated music book. Elementary/Late Elementary piano solos with teacher accompaniments. Songs: *Bali H'ai • Dites-Moi (Tell Me Why) • The Farmer and the Cowman • Getting to Know You • Happy Talk • I Whistle a Happy Tune • I'm Gonna Wash That Man Right Outa My Hair • If I Loved You • Oh, What a Beautiful Mornin' • Oklahoma • Shall We Dance? • Some Enchanted Evening • The Surrey with the Fringe on Top.*

00296613 Correlates with HLSPL Level 3 ....$12.95

Glee
arr. Jennifer Linn

Jennifer Linn provides intermediate-level solo arrangments of seven favorites from *Glee*: *Don't Stop Believin' • Endless Love • Imagine • Jump • Lean on Me • Proud Mary • True Colors.*

00296834 Correlates with HLSPL Level 5 ....$10.99

Elton John
arr. Carol Klose

8 classic Elton John songs arranged as intermediate solos: *Can You Feel the Love Tonight • Candle in the Wind • Crocodile Rock • Goodbye Yellow Brick Road • Sorry Seems to Be the Hardest Word • Tiny Dancer • Written in the Stars • Your Song.*

00296721 Correlates with HLSPL Level 5 ....$7.95

Joplin Ragtime Duets
arr. Fred Kern

Features full-sounding, intermediate-level arrangements for one piano, four hands of: *Heliotrope Bouquet • Magnetic March • Peacherine Rag • The Ragtime Dance.*

00296771 Correlates with HLSPL Level 5 ....$7.99

Jerome Kern Classics
arr. Eugénie Rocherolle

Intermediate level. Students young and old will relish these sensitive stylings of enduring classics: *All the Things You Are • Bill • Can't Help Lovin' Dat Man • I've Told Ev'ry Little Star • The Last Time I Saw Paris • Make Believe • Ol' Man River • Smoke Gets in Your Eyes • The Way You Look Tonight • Who?*

00296577 Correlates with HLSPL Level 5.......$12.99

Melody Times Two
Classic Counter-Melodies for Two Pianos, Four Hands
arr. Eugénie Rocherolle

This collection of classic counter-melody songs features four elegant and thoroughly entertaining arrangements for two pianos, four hands. Includes a definition and history of counter-melodies throughout musical periods; song histories; and composer biographies. The folio includes two complete scores for performance. Intermediate Level 4 Duos: *Baby, It's Cold Outside • Play a Simple Melody • Sam's Song • (I Wonder Why?) You're Just in Love.*

00296360 Intermediate Duets $12.95

Movie Favorites
arr. Fred Kern

Early-Intermediate/Intermediate piano solos. Songs: *Forrest Gump (Feather Theme) • Hakuna Matata • My Favorite Things • My Heart Will Go On • The Phantom of the Opera • Puttin' On the Ritz • Stand by Me.*

00296648 Correlates with HLSPL Levels 4/5 .....$6.99

Sing to the King
arr. Phillip Keveren

These expressive arrangements of popular contemporary Christian hits will inspire and delight intermediate-level pianists. Songs include: *By Our Love • Everlasting God • In Christ Alone • Revelation Song • Sing to the King • Your Name • and more.*

00296808 Correlates with HLSPL Level 5 ....$8.99

Sounds of Christmas (Volume 3)
arr. Rosemary Barrett Byers

Late Elementary/Early Intermediate level. For 1 piano/4 hands. Songs: *Blue Christmas • Christmas Is A-Comin' (May God Bless You) • I Saw Mommy Kissing Santa Claus • Merry Christmas, Darling • Shake Me I Rattle (Squeeze Me I Cry) • Silver Bells.*

00296615 Correlates with HLSPL Levels 3/4 .....$7.99

Today's Hits
arr. Mona Rejino

Intermediate-level piano solos. Songs: *Bless the Broken Road • Breakaway • Don't Know Why • Drops of Jupiter (Tell Me) • Home • Listen to Your Heart • She Will Be Loved • A Thousand Miles.*

00296646 Correlates with HLSPL Level 5...........$7.99

You Raise Me Up
arr. Deborah Brady

Contemporary Christian favorites. Elementary-level arrangements. Optional teacher accompaniments add harmonic richness. Songs: *All I Need • Forever • Open the Eyes of My Heart, Lord • We Bow Down • You Are So Good to Me • You Raise Me Up.*

00296576 Correlates with HLSPL Levels 2/3 .....$7.95

Visit our web site at **www.halleonard.com/hlspl.jsp** for all the newest titles in this series and other books in the Hal Leonard Student Piano Library.